Contents

I. THE HISTORICAL CONTEXT

Frantz Fanon's political theory is contained in four works: *Black Skin, White Masks* (1952), *Toward the African Revolution* (essays and papers written from 1952 to 1961), *A Dying Colonialism* (1959), and *The Wretched of the Earth* (1961). Together they total fewer than 900 pages. Yet Fanon deserves a place as one of the most profound political thinkers of the latter half of the twentieth century.[1] Although his influence among Euro-Americans has waned somewhat since the midseventies, Fanon has remained an important thinker in the Third World. His views on the catastrophic consequences for democracy, social justice, and equity resulting from the rule of the postcolonial nationalist elites are as current today as when he first expressed them. To argue that many in Europe and North America now dismiss his work as dated would be indicative of the very Eurocentrism Fanon so lucidly described.

The quarter century following 1945 was a period of extraordinary ferment and social upheaval, not only in what had been the colonized world but also within the core capitalist countries of Western Europe and North America, as well as the Stalinized socialist bloc. At various points the established social order was at least perceived to be under serious threat. If one can speak of a Zeitgeist it was that of liberation and human freedom, and Frantz Fanon was one of its most profound articulators.

Fanon, the son of a minor official in the civil service of the French colony of Martinique, was born in 1925. In 1942 he fled Vichy-dominated Martinique to join the Free French and was later wounded in the invasion of southern Europe, for which he received the Croix de Guerre. Returning home after the war, he took part in the successful Communist Party candidacy of his former teacher, the black writer Aimé Césaire, for a seat in the French General Assembly. In 1947 he went to France to study medicine and psychiatry. There he and thousands of demobilized soldiers and returning exiles joined large numbers of students and intellectuals from France's colonial empire at French universities. In this atmosphere Third World demands for national independence were a primary political and intellectual issue, and Fanon became deeply involved in African and West Indian student politics.

By far the dominant intellectual current in France in this period was Marxian and socialist. While many of the French intelligentsia never actually joined the Communist Party, a significant majority stood firmly on the left. This was underlined by the figure of Jean-Paul Sartre, France's most important postwar intellectual. Sartre, himself influenced by Kierkegaard, Nietzsche, Karl Jaspers, and Martin Heidegger, had interwoven existentialism with Marxism. All of these figures were important influences in Fanon's intellectual development, and existentialism's emphasis on human freedom and the individual's personal responsibility to make choices would become a recurring theme throughout Fanon's work. Sartre, who wrote the introduction to *The Wretched of the Earth;* his companion and fellow intellectual, Simone de Beauvoir; and Fanon later became close personal friends. Clearly Fanon was also affected by Marxism, from the writings of Marx and Engels to those of Lenin, Trotsky, Luxemburg, and Kautsky. Furthermore, he was familiar with the debates and political struggles that followed the Russian Revolution, as well as the trajectory of Soviet political and economic development.

Other important influences were the Franco-African–West Indian intellectuals associated with the literary-cultural movement known as *négritude,* the best known of whom were Fanon's mentor Césaire and the poet and, later, president of independent Senegal, Léopold Senghor. With regard to psychiatry, the most significant influence on Fanon was François Tosquelles, a leftist exile from Franco's Spain. Central to Tosquelles' theory was the insistence that mental illness develops within a social context and thus can only be understood and treated with this social framework in mind. Accordingly—and this theme is present in all Fanon's work, from his early days as a writer-psychiatrist to his death as a famous political theorist and revolutionary intellectual—Fanon wrote early in his career: "As a psychoanalyst, I should help my patient . . . to act in the direction of change in the social structure."[2]

In 1953 Fanon took a position as a psychiatrist at a government hospital in French Algeria. A year later the National Liberation Front (FLN) issued its Manifesto demanding independence. The French response was an all-out attempt to crush the rebellion. Fanon joined the FLN and began surreptitiously giving medical and psychiatric treatment to victims of French torture. In 1956, in a typically Fanonist burst of moral outrage, he resigned from government service in a letter to the resident minister:

> If psychiatry is the medical technique that aims to enable man no longer to be a stranger to his environment, I owe it to myself to affirm that the Arab, permanently an alien in his own country, lives in a state of absolute depersonalization. . . . The function of a social structure is to set up institutions to serve man's needs. A society that drives its members to desperate solutions is a non-viable society, a society to be replaced.[3]

Expelled from Algeria, Fanon went to FLN headquarters in neighboring independent Tunisia, where he began writing for its official organ, *El Moudjahid*. He also practiced psychiatry in several Tunisian facilities while simultaneously serving as a physician to FLN guerrillas. As a major international spokesman for the FLN, Fanon survived two French assassination attempts and an attempted abduction. In his travels he became personally familiar with all the leading voices of African nationalism. In late 1960 he was diagnosed with leukemia. He finished writing *The Wretched of the Earth* in the spring of 1961 and died that December. His body was slipped across the Algerian border for burial with full military honors in a liberated portion of the country.

II. HUMANIST AND RADICAL LIBERAL

Fanon's work first came to broad public attention in the early sixties as a consequence of the publication of his magnum opus, *The*

Wretched of the Earth, which David Caute has called "one of the great political documents of our time."[4] Crucial to Fanon's vision was the process by which the *individual* achieved self-liberation in and through the *collective* struggle. In his view, there was no tension between the individual and the collective. They were simply different aspects of the same human experience. The individual must go through a psychological, political, and cultural self-transformation in the *process* of creating collectively the new society. For Fanon this process was as important as the goals themselves. These two complementary facets interacted and created each other in the process of *becoming.* "An authentic national liberation," wrote Fanon, "exists only to the precise degree to which the individual has irreversibly begun his own liberation."[5] All politics must be the pursuit of the moral imperative. The major theme that permeates his writings is that of human freedom: "No attempt must be made to encase man, for it is his destiny to be set free."[6] His other subthemes—racism, colonialism, nationalism, class, violence, spontaneity, the revolutionary party, socialism—were subordinate to that one overriding demand: human freedom.

In philosophical terms, Fanon represents an attempt to return to a pre-Leninist idea of revolutionary socialism in which it was assumed by friend and foe alike that socialism represented an extension and deepening of democracy. In this conception only socialism could make substantive the promises of the older European traditions of secular humanism and radical liberalism; i.e., the centrality of human values and human worth, and respect for individual rights and freedoms. On the first page of *Black Skin, White Masks,* Fanon calls for a new humanism.[7] A moment later he adds, in an unmistakable allusion to and subtle criticism of Leninism, "and truly what is to be done is to set man free."[8] It could be argued that the man who wrote in such profoundly humanist terms in his first work was changed in fundamental ways by his later Algerian experiences. In the conclusion to *The Wretched,* he excoriates Europeans for their hypocrisy; they are never done talking of "Man" yet murder men everywhere.[9] Yet Fanon recognizes the European origins of liberal humanism and socialism, arguing that the solutions to humanity's problems have existed in European thought. Europeans have simply been unable to carry out the mission that befell them, human liberation.[10] Fanon then pleads, for the sake of humanity, that a new man be created.[11]

This fundamentally falls within the ambit of the humanist philosophical tradition and shows the degree to which Fanon was influenced by existentialism. Nor are these words mere "bookends" enclosing an essentially illiberal and antihumanist political philosophy. The theme of *Mankind's* liberation and ultimate human reconciliation permeates his work. Nowhere, even when his anger at European racism and violence is at its apogee, does he deviate. The conclusion to the famous chapter on violence in *The Wretched* renews the call for the rehabilitation of the *whole* of mankind, for which the help of the European people will be indispensable.[12]

As much as Fanon was a radical nationalist, he repeatedly insisted the nationalism he advocated was valid only within the context of the struggle against colonialism; it was a temporary tactic. With its goal accomplished, nationalism must be transformed into a higher consciousness, an inclusive internationalism. Mere nationalism could never provide a viable political program. It must be replaced by a *humanist* consciousness. Narrow, petty nationalism soon passes through chauvinism to racism and is incapable of implementing a program with a minimum of humanist content.[13]

Insofar as classical liberalism has always stood for the limited state and the separation of powers, Fanon was squarely within this tradition. He shared with that quintessential eighteenth-century liberal, Thomas Jefferson, a distrust of centralized government, a suspicion of the influence of the cities, and a deep respect for the rural producer. Fanon detested the centralized, one-party state. The only valid role for a political party was for it to be "a tool in the hands of the people" that informs the government of the policies that the people want implemented.[14]

Fanon also advocated, in the liberal tradition, a system of dispersed authority. The political leadership should not be concentrated in the capital but widely distributed geographically to stay in touch with the peoples' wishes. However, this system of governance should not be so diffuse as to compromise overall unity by encouraging internecine competition.[15] Implicit is a system in which there exists a creative and cooperative tension between the whole and the parts. There should be a strict separation between the parties and the government. Co-mingling the two functions leads to corruption of the party and careerism. At first glance this seems farfetched and even contradictory. How could the people rule, if their political wishes, expressed through their democratically chosen party leaders, could never be implemented by having them assume governmental power? However, there is no contradiction. Fanon's vision of political parties as mere transmission belts by which the people express their wishes is consistent with the idea of a separation of powers between the legislative and the executive. The parties assume a sort of legislative function; i.e., as "the tools of the people" they dominate the executive by informing it as to its tasks. In this scheme, the executive is no more than a group of technocrats who implement the people's will.

III. RACE AND CLASS

The linchpin of Fanon's theoretical structure was his insistence that race—of being the *other*—superseded class as the primary unit of analysis when dealing with the impact of colonialism on the Third World. However, the causes and effects of racism had fascinated (and appalled) him well before he became a revolutionary activist. He gives the subject fullest treatment in his first book, *Black Skin, White Masks,* published before he went to Algeria. The entire work is a compelling analysis of the dehumanizing nature of racism.

It is important to remember that Fanon was a psychiatrist *and* a black man. The racism he experienced personally and then studied intellectually imposed upon blacks a deep psychic shame and sense of inferiority. The black man, on the other hand, realizes:

> I am the slave not of the "idea" that others have of me but of my own appearance. . . . Shame. Shame and self-contempt. Nausea. When people like me, they tell me it is in spite of my color. When they dislike me, they point out that it is not because of my color. Either way, I am locked into the infernal circle.[16]

How can he begin to free himself from the enormous psychological burden thus imposed? This is the prescription Dr. Fanon gave himself as well as all black people:

I resolved . . . to assert myself as a BLACK MAN. Since the other hesitated to recognize me, there remained only one solution: to make myself known.[17]

Some forty years later, Stuart Hall, a West Indian intellectual, writes:

There are many writings about this question [the debilitating effects of racism on its victims], but for me the overwhelmingly powerful statement is to be found in Fanon's *Black Skin, White Masks,* for only in Fanon do you understand the internal traumas of identity which are the consequence of colonization and enslavement.[18]

It is with this analysis of racism and its formidable consequences that the psychiatrist-radical approached the colonial question and the struggle for national independence. As with the individual, so must an oppressed people assert themselves; they must break completely with the psychocultural as well as the political and economic dominance the invader imposes by force. The world of the colonized people as it existed was a world established by the outsider, those who came from elsewhere. It was a Manichaean world, a world starkly delimited by the reality of race:

This world divided into compartments, this world cut in two is inhabited by two different species. . . . The governing race is first and foremost those who come from elsewhere, those who are unlike the original inhabitants, "the others."

The settlers' town is a strongly built town, all made of stone and steel. It is a brightly lit town. . . . The town belonging to the colonized people . . . is a place of ill fame, peopled by men of evil repute. . . . It is a world without spaciousness; men live there on top of each other. . . . The native town is a hungry town, starved of bread, of meat, of shoes, of coal, of light. The native town is a crouching village, a town on its knees, a town wallowing in the mire. It is a town of niggers and dirty Arabs.[19]

With such powerful and evocative imagery Fanon describes the reality of colonization. Here the native is little more than an animal, but at the moment he begins to realize his own humanity, at that very moment, individually and as a people, the native begins to "sharpen the weapons with which he will secure its victory."[20] Fanon makes it clear here that the greatest weapon in the struggle for freedom is not a gun or a knife but one's own strongly asserted sense of humanity. It is here that the process of self-liberation begins.

Fanon attempts to abstract the essential character of colonialism. This was not to be found in the class categories he acknowledges were appropriate to an understanding of European societies.[21] Instead, the inner core of the colonial reality was to be found in what Fanon called race. The governing race included those who came from elsewhere and imposed their will through superior force upon the native, the nigger, the dirty Arab. What divided the world to which most of humanity had been consigned by European colonialism was not class, but

> the fact of belonging to or not belonging to a given race, a given species. In the colonies the economic substructure is also a superstructure. The cause is the consequence; you are rich because you are white, you are white because you are rich. This is why Marxist analysis should always be slightly stretched every time we have to do with the colonial problem.[22]

Fanon thus insisted that colonialism was more than simply a case of capitalists dominating and exploiting the labor of workers and peasants. At its basic level it was a question of one race dominating another, and the failure or reluctance of European socialists to understand this was just one more indication of a fundamental Eurocentrism.

IV. VIOLENCE

Unfortunately, Fanon, a descendant of African slaves turned revolutionary intellectual, was perceived by many as a dreaded apocalyptic advocate of violence, hatred, and black revenge. Many others, supporters of Third World revolutionary nationalism, have an equally narrow view of his work and, like his critics, have also tended to focus on his discussion of violence to the exclusion of the essential core of his thought. This has been unfortunate for two reasons: first, it has often obscured the far more important and essential elements of Fanon's thinking, parts of which are contained in the chapter entitled "Concerning Violence"; second, what Fanon did have to say about violence and the liberation struggle has often been extremely distorted and taken out of the broader context. Fanon is not simply accused of advocating the right to use physical force to overthrow colonialism along the lines of, say, Ho Chi Minh, Che Guevara, Nelson Mandela, or, even, George Washington. Instead he is said to have focused his entire work on the emotional, psychological, and political rewards that come from giving vent to an imputed primordial blood lust. Jack Woddis, for example, wrote, "Fanon, obsessed with violence, too glibly equates revolution with destruction."[23] The conservative, Eurocentric philosopher Hannah Arendt argued that Fanon, influenced by Sorel, "glorified violence for violence's sake."[24] She described French colonial policy as one of "restraint," despite its well-documented record of gratuitous brutality.[25] By doing so, she was able to make Fanon's arguments with regard to the right of revolution seem completely unreasonable.

Fanon's actual writing on violence is found in a seventy-two-page chapter in *The Wretched*. The evidence commonly cited to support the above claims are two sentences in which Fanon writes, "The colonized man finds his freedom in and through violence," and "At the level of individuals, violence is a cleansing force."[26] Those sentences are within a ten-page section in which Fanon defends the right of the oppressed to take up arms. The few earlier references to violence by the *native* are always in the more conventional sense. For example, writing almost as a clinical psychiatrist, Fanon deplores the aggression shown by the colonized toward one another. Elsewhere he suggests, "The starving peasant . . . is the first . . . to discover that only violence pays,"[27] but this is hardly an assertion of violence as a transcendental value. The violence discussed at length here is *the violence of the European against the colonized.* Using an evocative imagery Fanon exposes the nature of colonialism, seen as violence in its "natural state."[28] Consequently, the revolutionary violence Fanon justifies must be seen as one of *counterviolence,* a legitimate expression of self-defense. In the final twelve pages, subtitled "Violence in the International Context," Fanon is referring to the existing (then and now) *structural violence* of the international system.

Fanon uses the term *violence* in three separate but interconnected ways. First is the conventional language of common discourse, i.e., weapons and physical force with the consequence of death and injury. Fanon was convinced the French would never willingly give up Algeria. French bloodletting against Algerian resistance to occupation beginning in 1831 was well known. A century later it had, if anything, increased. At Sétif in 1945 peaceful demonstrations for independence resulted in the French slaughtering forty thousand Algerians in less than a month. At Mélouza three hundred Algerian males were rounded up and summarily executed. A decade prior to the American policy of "strategic hamlets" in Vietnam, the French engaged in wholesale population removals—a quarter of the population by 1959—in which entire villages were uprooted and forced into barbed-wire camps, where those who resisted were executed and many of the rest died of starvation and disease. White-settler militias surrounded and torched entire villages, murdering the inhabitants. These raids had no military purpose but were designed simply to terrorize the population into submission. Those who attack Fanon on violence would seem unaware of the scale of French savagery; ten percent of Algeria's Muslims were obliterated in the process of expelling the colonizer.[29] Restraint indeed!

The second sense in which Fanon used the term *violence* was to refer to the existing international system. The voracious expansion of European capitalism over a period of five hundred years had conquered and subdued the rest of the world and, in so doing, had created a certain set of international relationships: wealth and power centered in the white Euro-American homelands and poverty, hunger, and suffering elsewhere:

> The mass of the people . . . with their shrunken bellies outline what has been called a geography of hunger. It is an underdeveloped world, a world inhuman in its poverty. . . . Confronting this world, the European nations sprawl, ostentatiously opulent. This European opulence is literally scandalous, for it has been founded on slavery, it has been nourished with the blood of slaves.[30]

Finally, and most important, there is Fanon's metaphorical use of the terminology of violence to describe the process of cultural and racial debasement. In order to make themselves whole again, in order to regain the status of human being, the oppressed must reject the cultural order that has been imposed upon them. This absolute rejection of all that colonialism represented was itself a violent rupture; an act of *cultural* counterviolence. Only through radical and uncompromising action at the emotional and the political level could the black man—individually and collectively—begin to re-create himself and make himself truly human. It is useful here to look at the entire thought Fanon was expressing in one of those sentences for which he is criticized:

> At the level of individuals, violence is a cleansing force. It frees the native from his inferiority complex and from his despair and inaction; it makes him fearless and restores his self-respect. *Even if the armed struggle has been symbolic* and the nation is demobilized through a rapid movement of decolonization, the people have the time to see that the liberation has been the business of each and all and that the leader has no special merit.[31] (Italics added.)

With regard to the use of violence as a political weapon Fanon found himself mired deep in a moral dilemma. The history of European expansion in the Third World had shown him that whites were generally immune to arguments with regard to the rights of nonwhites. Europeans knew only one language: the language of force! If resistance were to be at all effective the colonized would have to employ in response the same tools that had been used to enslave him. There was, in Fanon's mind, an essential moral legitimacy to this response. Violence was a political reality, never a goal in itself. At the same time, Fanon was appalled by the violence that surrounded him.[32] While violence seemed politically justifiable and even necessary, he was deeply apprehensive about its actual use. He feared the possibility that the logic of violence would engulf and erode the moral sensibilities of those who had embarked on what was a morally legitimate crusade. By using the same physical violence against the slavemaster that had been used to enslave him, was not the slave descending to a similar level of barbarity and immorality? This was a dilemma with which Fanon grappled but was never able fully to resolve. Ultimately, he could do little more than say that violence in a just cause was legitimate but had to be used in the proper proportion. What that proportion was, when and how man slipped over the abyss, was unknowable.

V. CAPITALISM, CLASS, AND THE COLONY

Fanon could hardly be considered an "orthodox" Marxist; his comments on race stemmed most often from his use of psychiatric categories, and those on class from Marxist influences. The political-cultural milieu within which Fanon came of age intellectually was dominated by various "Marxisms." Fanon's comment about the need to "stretch" Marxist analysis when dealing with the colonized world illustrates this. One aspect of this "stretching," of course, was his emphasis on race as the dominant analytical paradigm when dealing with the colonies. This emphasis did not mean, however, that Fanon ignored class analysis, and it was his use of it, in addition to the racial dimension, that produced some of his most profound insights and predictions as to what could be foreseen in the coming postcolonial reality.

In Fanon's view the prototypical African colony in the fifties was divided into two fundamentally separate racial groups: the white European colonialist who came from elsewhere and the black or brown native.

1. The European

Other than his extensive discussion of the racial nature of European rule, little else is said about the European; Fanon makes no distinction between the administration, the army, the local representatives of the metropolitan French capital, the police, and the general settler community. The category "European" is a residual one including virtually everyone who is not a native. This is a flaw in Fanon's theoretical structure, as he often seems to be extrapolating from the Algerian experience and making broad generalizations about all colonies from that specific situation. He does not, for example, address why France was willing to negotiate a relatively peaceful withdrawal from the rest of its African colonies but violently resisted doing so in Algeria. One obvious explanation would be the role of a large, permanent European settler community. The struggles in Africa that witnessed the greatest violence and resistance to independence were precisely those where such an organized community existed.

2. The African

Fanon divided the indigenous population into four classes:

(*i*) *The Peasantry*

Fanon's view of the peasantry created the most controversy among orthodox leftists weaned on the classical Marxist understanding of the revolutionary role of the industrial proletariat. In Europe, capitalist expansion dissolved the peasantry of the Middle Ages and in its stead created an industrial proletariat—understood by Marx as a class of people who, from economic necessity, sold their labor power to capitalists in return for a wage. This class was seen by generations of Marxists as the historical class—the vast majority—that would take power and usher in the socialist epoch. In the Third World, however, capitalism had not functioned exactly the same way as in Europe. Peasant societies had been subjugated and incorporated into the capitalist world system, but as a class they had not been dissolved, i.e., turned into a class of landless wage laborers. This was particularly true in Africa, where only South Africa had created a large wage-laboring class—and even there the conversion was incomplete. Generally speaking, European colonial capitalism did not attempt to industrialize Africa. After nearly a century of colonialism, the continent as a whole still had a vast peasant majority and a very small wage-laboring class concentrated in the colonial capitals.

How then could one speak in Marxist terms of a proletarian-led socialist revolution in a mainly agrarian society? Marxists struggled with this problem and addressed it in various ways. Common to all solutions, however, was an insistence that their various revolutions be led by a Communist Party that was dominated by a working-class ideology and that would elevate those minuscule working classes to the status of the leading class—the essential Leninist formulation. Fanon implicitly rejected these arguments as an attempt to force sociopolitical realities into a pre-existing formula that had become mere dogma. Imposing categories and concepts Fanon acknowledged as appropriate to Europe on situations where they were manifestly inapplicable was simply another form of Eurocentrism.

The answer was simple! If there were to be a socialist revolution in Africa the peasantry would have to be the leading class because it was the vast majority, because it was the most oppressed, and, finally, because it would benefit the most from socialism. Nor did Fanon have sympathy for those socialists who argued that colonial countries were not ripe for socialism because they were technologically backward and must first pass through developed capitalism:

> The theoretical question that for the last fifty years has been raised whenever the history of underdeveloped countries is under discussion—whether or not the bourgeois stage can be skipped— ought to be answered in the field of revolutionary action, and not by logic.[33]

Fanon attributed to the peasantry as a whole qualities of wisdom, morality, revolutionary discipline, and unity of action it clearly did not show. In his defense, one must note that classical Marxism made the same mistake regarding the working class.

(ii) The Lumpenproletariat

Fanon's choice of this term, with its extremely negative connotations in the context of European history, was a poor one. In part, one suspects, he was motivated by his disdain for much of the organized European left, in particular because of France's refusal to accept absolutely the colonized peoples' right to independence. The European left carried the same deeply imbued sense of racial and cultural superiority as did most other Europeans. Black people were like children, deserving independence perhaps, but not without the tutelage of European intellectuals. Fanon, cognizant of the power of words, knew full well that ascribing positive, revolutionary qualities to a class fraction called the lumpenproletariat would certainly infuriate the orthodox.

Despite maintaining the peasantry, colonialism had transformed traditional land tenure, displacing large numbers whose only recourse was to migrate to the outskirts of the cities, where they lived in hovels. With no access to regular employment, this newly urbanized class eked out an existence through a wide variety of economic pursuits, from casual and migrant labor, to petty trading and domestic service, to crime and prostitution. These people were displaced by the system, victimized by racism, and forced to live what was at best a tenuous existence; it was among them, Fanon felt, that "the rebellion will find its urban spearhead," which would complement that vast, peasant-based rural uprising he envisioned. The colonial lumpenproletariat was, he wrote, "one of the most spontaneous and the most radically revolutionary forces of a colonized people."[34]

Marx was scathing in his comments regarding the European lumpenproletariat in nineteenth-century urban Europe. He referred to them, a minority, as scum, a rotting mass, vagabonds, thieves, criminals, and so on. This was not so in the colonial city described by Fanon. Fanon's lumpenproletariat were migrant workers, casual and day laborers, the unemployed. His purpose was to distinguish them from the small and better-off group of indigenous workers engaged in regular, skilled, full-time employment. Fanon's leftist critics also ignore the patriotic appeal that Marx wrote was essential to the state's recruitment of the lumpenproletariat as a force to be used against the organized working class. The French lumpenproletariat was, after all, French; the German, German; and the English, English. They could respond to patriotic appeals. In the colonies, the class that Fanon was calling the "urban spearhead" was made up, first and foremost, of natives—the victims of invasion, racism, and exploitation. These were the people who wore no shoes and lived in hovels, who envied the settler. These were the people of the hungry town, the town on its knees wallowing in the mire. They were not subject to patriotic appeals, willing to give their lives for the French Republic.

(*iii*) *The Working Class*

Whereas conventional Marxism ascribed revolutionary potential to the working class, Fanon took a distinctly different position. He maintained, as he had so often proclaimed elsewhere, that the colonial system itself made things different. In the colonies the working class was comparatively well off; Fanon unfortunately used the word "pampered," which allowed critics to focus on a single word and so avoid the larger analytical point he was making. He was specific about what he meant by the working class: industrial workers, miners, dockers, tram conductors, taxi drivers, interpreters, and nurses, i.e., those engaged in regular, full-time, skilled wage labor.[35] Fanon saw in this small and embryonic working class a general tendency to protect its positions while simultaneously trying to advance through a moderate nationalism. Its members cast their lot with the moderate nationalism of the Westernized native intellectual and professional class and were interested not, argued Fanon, in a fundamental revolutionary change but merely in improving their already relatively better position. Their political instincts would lead them to accept compromise and neocolonialism, not the revolutionary socialism that alone could bring justice.

(*iv*) *The National Middle Class*

In many ways his analysis of the postcolonial nationalist elite is the high point of Fanon's intellectual achievement. References are scattered throughout his work, but in the third chapter of *The Wretched*, "The Pitfalls of National Consciousness," Fanon brings his entire argument together in a devastating and prescient critique that effectively describes the trajectory of postcolonial Africa. If one went to sleep knowing the Africa of 1961, awakened to find the devastation that Africa has become in 1995, and wanted to find out what had happened, one could start in no better a place than these fifty-eight pages. Edward Said, a prominent literary scholar and critic, has referred to Fanon as a "true prophetic genius," the first major theorist who understood that orthodox nationalism only appears to give authority to the nationalist bourgeoisie, while in fact it extends and strengthens imperialism's hegemony.[36]

Two things must be kept in mind when reading Fanon's critique of the national middle class, the emerging state class that in 1960–61 was only on the threshold of power. First, it was exactly what it appeared to be; i.e., he had become familiar with the political class—backgrounds, political organizations, thinking—that was just then assuming power, and he anticipated with dread and extraordinary foresight what a tragedy it would make of independent Africa. There is, however, a second, more subtle theme. Fanon, like many African nationalists, was a socialist. Most African socialists were convinced that a radical break with the international capitalist system was an absolute precondition to the establishment of real independence and a regime of justice. The general model for such a "noncapitalist" road was the Soviet Union, which, it should be remembered, was undergoing an extraordinary period of growth between 1950 and 1965. Fanon, however, understood far more clearly than most the dangers of this type of thinking and the deep flaws inherent in the Soviet model. Thus, one must read Fanon here as critiquing not only the emerging state class in Africa but state classes elsewhere that claimed to be building socialism.

Fanon was unsparing in his contempt for the national middle class. It was a mere caricature of the European bourgeoisie, after which it so slavishly modeled itself. Under the colonial system the middle class had gained a European-style education, a certain status, and moderate economic and political advancement. They had rejected their own culture and adopted that of the occupiers. They had become civilized, European! Yet in the eyes of the European they would forever remain mere natives. The consequence was a deep resentment against the very people they tried so hard to emulate. Prevented by the colonial system's inherent racism from advancing beyond a certain point, the Westernized elite were the first to begin organized nationalist agitation. However, they missed the opportunity to create a broad-based national movement because their essentially European mentality had taught them to distrust the vast majority of their countrymen—the rural masses who were ripe for organization and deeply hated the colonial system. The primary goal of the native elite was not to benefit the whole people but simply to displace the European so that they might have a greater share of the spoils of exploitation:

Yet the national middle class constantly demands the nationalization of the economy and of the trading sectors. This is because,
from their point of view, nationalization does not mean placing
the whole economy at the service of the nation and deciding to
satisfy the needs of the nation. For them, nationalization does
not mean governing the state with regard to the new social relations whose growth it has been decided to encourage. To them,
nationalization quite simply means the transfer into native hands
of those unfair advantages which are the legacy of the colonial
period.[37]

Fanon argued that the nationalist bourgeoisie was economically
and politically underdeveloped. The rising bourgeois middle classes
of early modern Europe had historically served a progressive function. Their insistence upon innovation and capital accumulation had
broken the fetters of feudalism and brought about modernization.
The native middle classes in the colonies were incapable of initiat-
ing such a progressive process. Where the European bourgeois had
been "captains of industry," the native middle classes were mere
petty-minded traders:

> In the underdeveloped countries, we have seen that no true bour-
> geoisie exists; there is only a sort of little greedy caste, avid and
> voracious, with the mind of a huckster, only too glad to accept
> the dividends that the former colonial power hands out to it.[38]

Incapable of implementing a program that would benefit the whole
people, of replicating the historically progressive role of the rising
bourgeoisie in Europe, because of their petty greed the Westernized
elite was also unwilling to place themselves and their intellectual
resources at the disposal of the masses to create a progressive socialist program. Consequently, they discovered their true historical
mission: that of "intermediary," of being the mere "business agent"
of European imperialism.[39]

The masses had been promised that independence would bring
a radical transformation in their lives, but soon this hope turned to
disillusionment, resentment, and opposition. To maintain their
newly acquired privileges the nationalist elite in control of the state

engages in a petty nationalism that degenerates into chauvinism and, eventually, tribalism. First citizens from other African countries, then citizens from other ethnic groups are made scapegoats by the unscrupulous leadership for the disasters that have befallen the nation. Unable to contain the rising discontent, the new state class begins to undermine the newly won political freedoms that had been a consequence of the anticolonial movement:

> The bourgeoisie chooses the solution that seems to it the easiest, that of the single party. . . . The single party is the modern form of the dictatorship of the bourgeoisie, unmasked, unpainted, unscrupulous, and cynical.[40]

A personality cult develops in which supreme leadership is invested in someone who had once been a hero of the movement. The masses begin to realize that treason has been committed as they sink further into stagnation, poverty, and resentment. Radicals who had advocated a truly revolutionary socialist transformation are eliminated. The party becomes a mere shell of what it had been and begins to serve only as a vehicle for career advancement and as an implement of coercion. Eventually police and military power become the arbiters of politics, and the dictatorship is implemented.

The "personality cult" as an African political phenomenon was barely emergent; perhaps then it was only partially applicable to Nasser in Egypt, Nkrumah in Ghana, and Touré in Guinea. The subtle point of Fanon's critique can be understood in the context of the years immediately following the Bolshevik Revolution. The Constituent Assembly was abolished after a free election failed to give the Bolsheviks the majority. Dissent grew as many objected to the course the revolution was taking. They were silenced. Within a few years all other socialist parties were abolished. In a short time even dissent within the Bolshevik Party was forbidden, and the party degenerated. Soon, under Stalin, two "personality cults" developed: one for the great leader himself (and in reference to whom the term *personality cult* was coined) and another surrounding the dead Lenin. Ultimately, force became the political arbiter in the Soviet Union.

VI. GENDER, RACE, AND COLONIALISM

The considerable attention Fanon paid to the "women's question" is extraordinary, if for no other reason than for its time. In the immediate postwar period virtually no one writing on decolonization or political theory in general paid much attention to the specific problems relating to women. There were, to be sure, comments on gender, but they tended to be at best tangential to the primary question, i.e., the revolution either as class-based or as a nationalist phenomenon, or both. Oppression of women was seen not as a special form of subjugation but rather as one that was subsumed in the general category of class or national oppression.

In those instances where it was implicitly or explicitly conceded that women faced a unique, gender-specific form of oppression, the issue was generally seen as being either "divisive" or a "distraction" in the context of the larger, more important struggle. This argument was put forward by the male leadership of many liberation movements: we must wait until after the revolution before addressing it. During the fifties the only writers dealing with gender oppression at all were feminists, for whom that specific subject was the major area of concern. It is interesting that Fanon was a close personal friend of Simone de Beauvoir's, a prominent member of that first generation of postwar feminists.

Sprinkled throughout Fanon's work are comments recognizing women as victims of a distinctive form of oppression, but his specific thoughts on gender are contained in four chapters in two books, *Black Skin, White Masks* and *A Dying Colonialism*. In the former, Fanon's particular concern is as a psychiatrist (he had just finished his training) looking at the intersection of race and erotic desire. Racial oppression and racial self-hatred rather than gender oppression per se are paramount. Here we will concentrate more on Fanon's discussion of the process by which gender oppression is addressed within the ongoing context of revolution. He does this in two chapters in *A Dying Colonialism*: "Algeria Unveiled" and "The Algerian Family." There should be no question that the Fanonist discourse in general sees the abstract revolutionary as being primarily a male. However, here he examines the mechanisms by which "traditional" gender-based roles begin to break down. While Fanon is notable in

> "The writing of Malcom X or Eldridge Cleaver or Amiri Baraka or the Black Panther leaders reveals how profoundly they have been moved by the thoughts of Frantz Fanon." —THE BOSTON GLOBE

Psychiatrist, humanist, revolutionary, Frantz Fanon was one of the great political analysts of our time. His work has had a major impact on civil rights, anticolonial, and black consciousness movements around the world.

THE WRETCHED OF THE EARTH.

PREFACE BY JEAN-PAUL SARTRE; TRANSLATED FROM THE FRENCH BY CONSTANCE FARRINGTON. *The Wretched of the Earth*, Fanon's classic work of modern revolutionary theory, concerns the psychology of the colonized and their path to liberation. It reflects a people's outrage and frustration, but it is more than a diatribe against Western colonialism. A brilliant and impassioned examination of the role of violence in effecting historical change, *The Wretched of the Earth* is a veritable handbook of social reorganization for leaders of emerging nations and is necessary reading for anyone who wants to understand the psychology of the oppressed.

Paper • 0-8021-5083-7 • $12 • 316 pp.

BLACK SKIN, WHITE MASKS.

TRANSLATED FROM THE FRENCH BY CHARLES LAM MARKMANN. *Black Skin, White Masks* is the unsurpassed study of the black psyche in a white world. Hailed for its scientific analysis and poetic grace when it was first pub-

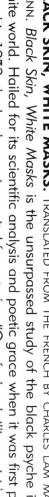

ORDER FORM

SCHOOL

NAME AND POSITION

DEPARTMENT

ADDRESS

CITY _____ STATE _____ ZIP CODE

TOTAL FOR BOOKS

POSTAGE AND HANDLING AND SALES TAX

(POSTAGE: $4.00 for 1st book, 75¢ for each additional)

TOTAL AMOUNT ENCLOSED

☐ I HAVE INCLUDED MY CHECK OR MONEY ORDER FOR THE FULL AMOUNT DUE, MADE PAYABLE TO GROVE/ATLANTIC, INC.

☐ CHARGE MY CREDIT CARD: ____ MASTERCARD ____ VISA ____ AMEX

PRICE LIST

ISBN Prefix: 0-8021-

☐ THE WRETCHED OF THE EARTH

  5083-7 $12

☐ BLACK SKIN, WHITE MASKS

  5084-5 $12

☐ A DYING COLONIALISM

  5027-6 $12

☐ TOWARD THE AFRICAN REVOLUTION

  3090-7 $8.95

SIGNATURE

PLEASE ALLOW 4–6 WEEKS FOR DELIVERY

Send your order to:

Grove/Atlantic, Inc.   841 Broadway   New York, NY 10003

PLEASE COMPLETE THE FOLLOWING FOR EXAM COPY REQUESTS

COURSE TITLE

BEGINNING DATE

COLLEGE STORE NAME

ACADEMIC EXAMINATION AND DESK COPY POLICY

Paperback examination and desk copies are available to professors and teachers considering a title for course adoption. All requests must be submitted in writing using the above order form or on university letterhead or the appropriate AAUP form. All requests must include the course's title, beginning date, and approximate enrollment size, as well as the name of the college store that will be placing the order. Please include your school address. Books will not be shipped to your home address. To help defray shipping and handling charges, $4.00 for the first book and 75¢ for each additional book ordered must accompany your request.

with a whole range of words and images. . . . Yet it is Fanon the man, rather than the medical specialist or intellectual, who makes the book so hard to put down."
—Robert Coles, THE NEW YORK TIMES BOOK REVIEW

Paper • 0-8021-5084-5 • $12 • 232 pp.

A DYING COLONIALISM. WITH AN INTRODUCTION BY ADOLFO GILLY; TRANSLATED FROM THE FRENCH BY HAAKON CHEVALIER.

A *Dying Colonialism* is Fanon's incisive and illuminating account of how, during the Algerian Revolution, the peoples of Algeria changed centuries-old cultural patterns and embraced certain ancient cultural practices long derided by their colonialist oppressors. Fanon uses the fifth year of the revolution as a point of departure for an explication of the inevitable dynamics of colonial oppression. This is a strong, lucid, and militant book; to read it is to understand why Fanon says that for the colonized, "having a gun is the only chance you still have of giving a meaning to your death."

Paper • 0-8021-5027-6 • $12 • 181 pp.

TOWARD THE AFRICAN REVOLUTION: Political Essays. TRANSLATED FROM THE FRENCH BY HAAKON CHEVALIER.

Toward the African Revolution is a powerful collection of articles, essays, and letters, many of them originally published in the Algerian National Liberation Front underground newspaper *El Moudjahid*, that allows us to trace the development of Fanon's thoughts during the nine years prior to his death. Taken together, they constitute a portrait of a brilliant mind in constant evolution, fired by outrage and a passion for human dignity, relentlessly refining ideas to the flashpoint in the crucible of revolutionary praxis. "His writing is as stylistically powerful and intellectually compelling as that of Thomas Paine. Yet, the purpose of these essays is not so much to incite revolt as to explain it. . . . Should be of great interest to anyone studying colonialism, nationalism, and the currents of the Afro-Asian world." —CHOICE

Paper • 0-8021-3090-7 • $8.95 • 197 pp.

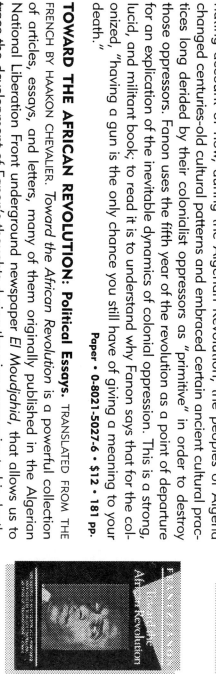

Grove Press books are distributed by Publishers Group West. The complete works of Frantz Fanon are available at fine bookstores everywhere or can be ordered directly from Grove Press at (800) 788-3123.

that he does not see the oppression of women as simply a facet of the larger class and national oppression (although these aspects are clearly interwoven), he does argue that its dissolution begins in the general ongoing progress of the revolution itself.

Fanon points out that women in Algerian society have been traditionally under the complete dominance of men: fathers, husbands, brothers. Furthermore, these traditions—variously termed regressive, reactionary, feudal—oppress women. Any movement that makes a claim to be establishing a just society must adopt new attitudes with regard to women. Traditionally the veil has, indeed, been symbolic of male control over women. However, as elsewhere, national oppression and racism as represented by colonialism casts a slightly different light on the question. Despite the social origins of the veil embedded in the repression of women, the custom has taken on additional meaning. French colonial policy, to increase control, was in part predicated upon the destruction of Arab culture. One aspect of this was for the French to label the veil repressive. Consequently, in the interwar years they began a campaign to discourage its use. Viewed as an attack on indigenous culture, the response was a "bristling" resistance. Even if the values of the French in this regard were objectively progressive, Fanon points out, the overall response was to reject them precisely because of their origins.

Until 1955 the revolution was completely male, Fanon explains, but the very requirements of the struggle eroded the traditional constraints placed upon Algerian women. French repression made it necessary that women be incorporated into the revolutionary organization. Fanon makes it clear that the decision to do so was also the consequence of the demands of Algerian women. They too had a stake in the nation's liberation and should be integrally involved in its attainment. The revolutionary tasks assigned to and accomplished by women began to change the way they were perceived by their male comrades. In her advances the male begins to find his own liberation from the constraints of gender-imposed roles: "The militant man discovers the militant woman, and jointly they create new dimensions for Algerian society."[41]

The particular conditions forced upon the people in their defense of the nation caused the family as it had been traditionally structured to break down. Individual family members began to make their own decisions instead of trusting to entrenched patriarchal customs revolving around the role of the father and husband, in particular, and the elders, in general. The diminution of patriarchal power by the forces unleashed by the revolution could not help but change prevailing family relations. Taken literally, of course, what Fanon writes about the Algerian Revolution and the changing roles of women can only be seen as a vast exaggeration, another example of his enduring utopianism. What he describes did not take place during the revolution itself or in the early days of postindependence construction; in fact, it never became substantially more than a rhetorical commitment on the part of the male-dominated state. Fanon had obviously hoped that the Algerian Revolution would proceed forward to establish a regime of justice and would, furthermore, serve as a model for the rest of the world. In that hope he was disappointed. However, as elsewhere in his work, the discussion of a transformation in gender roles must be seen as more than a description of an actual event—as a normative appeal, an idealized vision of what *could* be if the opportunities created by actual events were acted upon.

Fanon reminds us of his continuing relevance by giving us a tool with which to gain an insight into part of what motivates the fundamentalist movement that convulsed Algeria almost four decades after his death. The national middle class, neither prepared for nor capable of transcending petty nationalism, betrayed the revolution. The development that took place after Algerian independence benefited primarily the national bourgeoisie that is now barely clinging to power through the use of naked force. Many have responded by retreating into a mystical and largely invented religious tradition. Of these, some have tried to re-impose control over women through blatant terrorism.

VII. FANON'S SOCIALISM AND COMMUNIST ORTHODOXY

Fanon's immediate political concern was the African Revolution, of which he saw the Algerian experience as a model—both positive and negative. It was toward Africa and Algeria that his analyses and prescriptions were primarily directed. Nowhere in his work is there an explicit evaluation of communist societies. There are two obvious, interrelated reasons. First, Fanon was writing at the very height of the Cold War. Third World countries were caught in the vice of the East-West conflict, each side demanding allegiance as the price of support. The FLN was carrying on a brutal war with a key NATO member. This prevented other NATO members and their wider spheres of influence, whatever their diverse inclinations may have been, from giving all but the most limited support to the Algerians. Consequently, in seeking outside help, the FLN had no alternative but to cultivate its relations with the Soviet bloc. This international political reality precluded Fanon from any directly negative comments regarding orthodox communism.

There was also the internal political configuration of the FLN. Fanon belonged to the FLN's left wing. However, that wing itself had various factions. Among them were those like Fanon who sought a radically democratic and decentralized socialism, as well as a "pro-Soviet" component. In his effort to push the FLN generally to the left, Fanon could hardly have wished to alienate potential allies in the left wing by openly attacking the model they admired. Consequently, it had to be done through the use of allusion and implication, necessarily oblique references. For example, Fanon attacked political dictatorship and governments that demand "obedience and discipline" with the following observation:

> That *famous dictatorship,* whose supporters believe that it is called for by the *historical process* and consider it an indispensable prelude to the dawn of independence, in fact symbolizes the decision of the bourgeois caste to govern the underdeveloped country first with the help of the people, but soon against them. . . . The incoherent mass of the people is seen as a blind force that must be continually held in check either by mystification or by the fear inspired by the police force. . . . In these conditions, you may be sure, the party is unchallenged and 99.99% of the votes are cast for the government candidate.[42] (Italics added.)

There should be no doubt as to which famous dictatorship Fanon is alluding here. Lenin often used precisely that terminology to defend his notion of the "dictatorship of the proletariat," which was necessitated by the "historical process."

Fanon only mentioned communist countries directly in the context of the Cold War, which he argued had an overall negative effect on the Third World. He derided the Western obsession that found communism the culprit behind all nationalist struggles. However, his remarks very subtly reveal his own ambivalence to both East and West:

> Americans should be told that if they want to fight communism they must, in certain sectors, adopt Communist attitudes. For colonial peoples enslaved by Western nations, the Communist countries are the only ones that have on all occasions taken their defense. The colonized countries need not concern themselves to find out whether this attitude is dictated by the interests of Communist strategy; they note first of all that this general behavior is to their interest.
>
> The colonial peoples are not particularly communistic, but they are irreducibly anti-colonialist.
>
> They will not choose the United States because they are afraid of communism, but because their attitude in the great problems that shake the world—in this case the problems of decolonization—will conform to a spirit of solidarity, of equity, and of authentic justice.[43]

There was much Fanon was saying here. To fight communism the Americans must, *in certain sectors*, adopt communist attitudes. Which communist attitudes? Which sectors? An essential one was support for independence. The communist countries had consistently done so. Furthermore, it was legitimate for anticolonial movements to accept help from whomever offered it. However, Fanon was also intimating he was under no illusions as to the reasons for this general communist support, i.e., strategic self-interest rather than any principled internationalism. Why did Fanon find it necessary to say the colonized peoples were not particularly communistic? Fanon had consistently left no doubt as to his own socialism as well as his conviction that the colonized peoples felt the same; only with the demise of capitalism and the advent of socialism could a truly just society be established. He could only have been drawing a distinction between the kind of radically democratic socialism he proposed and that which *actually existed*, known as communism. Here he was cautioning his comrades not to follow what he undoubtedly felt was a false, if nominally attractive, model. And what of the United States and the West? The colonized peoples would choose America with regard to its support for *solidarity, equity,* and *authentic justice*. To Fanon these words were not merely empty slogans; they represented an actual moral commitment and policy. For Fanon it was self-evident: only through embracing a radically democratic socialism could equity and authentic justice be realized.

Fanon believed that when a party assumes total power and tolerates no opposition a barrier is raised between state and society. The party becomes a mere shell and, instead of stimulating mass involvement, has as its chief function that of immobilizing the people, of depriving them of political and social involvement:

> The living party, which ought to make possible the free exchange of ideas which have been elaborated according to the real needs of the mass of the people, has been transformed into a trade union of individual interests. . . . Today, the party's mission is to deliver to the people the instructions which issue from the summit. There no longer exists the fruitful give-and-take from the bottom to the top and from the top to the bottom which creates and guarantees democracy in a party.[44]

Some committed radicals struggle for a living socialism that includes popular participation, but they are soon neutralized and excluded from positions of influence. Corruption and a decline in public morals become commonplace. Political education degenerates into mere sloganizing and the people are treated like children. The state never stops reminding them that

> the direction of affairs by a strong authority, in other words a dictatorship, is a necessity. . . . The party . . . controls the masses . . . to remind them constantly that the government expects from them obedience and discipline.[45]

What Fanon has here described regarding the degeneration of the party is redolent of what happened with all Leninist parties. Over and over Fanon held fast to his belief that the common people could participate in the decisions that determine the nation's direction. The people can understand all problems rendered in everyday language: "Everything can be explained to the people, on the single condition that you really want them to understand."[46] Socialism for Fanon was first and foremost a moral imperative. Mere caricatures of socialism, the communist regimes of Eastern Europe were as degrading to the people as were the decadent capitalist countries of Euro-America:

> [T]he choice of a socialist regime, a regime which is completely oriented toward the will of the people as a whole and based on the principle that man is the most precious of all possessions, will allow us to go forward more quickly and more harmoniously, and thus make impossible that caricature of society where all economic and political power is held in the hands of a few who regard the nation as a whole with scorn and contempt.[47]

VIII. CONCLUSION

In several ways the evolution of postcolonial societies over the last forty years has rendered obsolete some aspects of Fanon's thinking with regard to both race and class in Third World countries. The mere fact of political independence has changed significantly the manner in which race remains a factor internationally; i.e., there is no longer the legal fact of being a European possession, as colonial administrations and settler communities of European origin whose prerogatives were determined by that origin are a thing of the past. This should not be understood to say, however, that Fanon's views with regard to the importance of race and the international political system are no longer relevant. Race and immigration are now significant issues tied to growing efforts by Euro-America to seal itself off from the "nonwhite hordes" it imagines are trying to overrun it. With the collapse of the communist "enemy" there appears to be a frantic search for a new one, and this increasingly seems to be taking the form of racial, national, ethnic, and cultural terminology— what a prominent American intellectual has unfortunately labeled the coming "clash of civilizations."[48] Clearly Fanon's insistence upon recognizing the reality of the racial dimension and its danger to the survival of humanity is as relevant now as it was at midcentury.

Fanon's influence in the United States and Europe began to wane in the seventies. The themes of justice and human liberation he put forward with such eloquence have become lost in the cynicism and greed of the last twenty years. Many of those who once found inspiration in the idea that human beings could make the common world they share a better place—a "regime of justice" in Fanon's words—fell victim to the cynicism of that old canard: "If you're not a socialist at twenty you have no heart. If you're still a socialist at fifty you have no brains."

Fanon represented a period of optimism in which the Zeitgeist demanding freedom was felt by many to be within the realm of human possibility. In some ways, the cutting-edge civil rights organization of the 1960s—the Student Nonviolent Coordinating Committee—was an American reflection of Fanon's thinking and deeply felt belief in the capacity of the most oppressed to take control of their lives and achieve justice. This is not to say that SNCC organizers were influenced directly by Fanon. In the early sixties, only a few had read *The Wretched of the Earth* in French, before its English translation a few years later. Yet early SNCC thinking regarding the relationship between organizer and organized and the methods they used embodied Fanon's ideas. SNCC workers in the rural South from 1961 to 1966 most often circumvented the established leadership and, instead, insisted that the most oppressed among us were capable of participating in the decisions that affect their lives. Perhaps the high point of this was the appearance at the Democratic National Convention in Atlantic City in August 1964 of a delegation of poor, black Mississippians who believed in real democracy. Sharecroppers, tenant farmers, workers—some barely literate—held much of the nation transfixed for a few days as they profoundly and eloquently spoke of democracy and justice and challenged directly the entrenched American party system. These were the poor leading themselves, a consequence of Fanon's "potent mixture." This was obviously not a "revolutionary situation" in the sense that Fanon used it or in the way that term is normally understood. But in the context of the history of black Americans it was indeed revolutionary. For a short time the underpinnings of the world's most powerful nation were shaken.

Emma Goldman, the famous turn-of-the-century American Marxist-anarchist, went to the Soviet Union shortly after the October Revolution. She cringed at what she saw: the rise of an authoritarian, centralized, antidemocratic state calling itself socialist. In the early 1920s she wrote home despairingly of her disappointment to her close friend and fellow anarchist, Alexander Berkman. Berkman replied that she was expecting too much, too soon. Revolutions take centuries to deliver on their promises. He pointed to the French Revolution—liberty, equality, and fraternity—and suggested that, over a century later, it still had not delivered completely on those promises.

Recently, Edward Said has mentioned a "disappointment in the politics of liberation" and "the disenchantment with the Third World that overtook so many people during the 1970s and 1980s."[49] Said was particularly referring to one-time left-wing intellectuals who had placed so much faith in the hope that the Third World would supersede decadent Euro-America and produce an immediate paradise. They had failed to heed Fanon's comments regarding the strength of global capitalism and the nature of the political class that was coming to power in the former colonies. It was easier to blame the venal and bloodthirsty dictatorships that followed on Africans alone. The combination of Western moneylenders and obsessed cold warriors who helped keep these dictators in place was conveniently forgotten. Euro-American intellectuals turned self-indulgently inward. There was no more hope!

As long as Frantz Fanon can be pigeonholed as merely a theorist of radical, nationalist revolution in the Third World the essential truth of his work can be ignored. After all, the colonial world as it was at midcentury is gone. In the sterile, legal sense virtually the entire world is made up of legally sovereign states. The "evil empire" of communist dictatorship has been defeated. The American Francis Fukuyama has proclaimed the "end of history," by which he means the ultimate victory of free-market, liberal capitalism. Yet the Third World retains the characteristics that Fanon described as a "geography of hunger." And this hunger is not simply confined to what used to be the colonial world. Significant parts of the former Second World—the one-time communist bloc—are fast in its grip. More and more, in fact, even the industrialized West—the First World—is characterized by a growing polarization of wealth and poverty. With the demise of the communist alternative, working people in the rich industrialized countries are being told they must be "realistic." The so-called social safety net must be sacrificed to an impersonal god called competitiveness. High-paying jobs are either disappearing or being exported to low-wage areas, but hardly in the quantity that would employ sufficient numbers of Third World poor. Simultaneously, the world's poor, in what is shaping up as the largest migration in human history, are now knocking at the doors of a fortress called Euro-America, which is desperately trying to keep them out. Emma Lazarus's famous line about giving us the tired, the poor, the huddled masses yearning to breathe free is now an empty promise, fit only for a plaque at the foot of a monument or for elementary school children to memorize as part of a history lesson. Fanon's words about racism, poverty, dispossession, and alienation are as relevant today as they ever were. It is ironic indeed that a man who spoke so often of human reconciliation is so strongly identified with the idea of violence and retribution. Fanon was much more than merely a voice for black people. He was also a spokesman for humanity. He insisted it was man's destiny to be free. Humanity has yet to reach its destiny.

Notes

1. A small portion of this essay appeared previously in German in William W. Hansen and Brigitte H. Schulz, "Kolonialer Kapitalismus und Sozialismus: Die radikale Theorie des Frantz Fanon," in Theodor Bergmann and Mario Kessler, eds., "*Ketzer im Kommunismus: Alternativen zum Stalinismus* (Mainz: Decaton Verlag, 1993). Permission for its use has been granted.
2. *Black Skin, White Masks,* p. 100.
3. *Toward the African Revolution,* p. 53.
4. Caute, p. 68.
5. *Toward the African Revolution,* p. 103.
6. *Black Skin, White Masks,* p. 230.
7. *Black Skin, White Masks,* p. 7.
8. *Black Skin, White Masks,* p. 9.
9. *The Wretched of the Earth,* p. 311.
10. *The Wretched of the Earth,* pp. 313, 314.
11. *The Wretched of the Earth,* pp. 314–16.
12. *The Wretched of the Earth,* p. 106.
13. *The Wretched of the Earth,* pp. 156, 163, 203, 204.
14. *The Wretched of the Earth,* p. 185.
15. *The Wretched of the Earth,* pp. 185, 186.
16. *Black Skin, White Masks,* p. 116.
17. *Black Skin, White Masks,* p. 115.
18. Hall, p. 8. (See under "Related Works.")
19. *The Wretched of the Earth,* pp. 39–40.
20. *The Wretched of the Earth,* p. 43.
21. *Toward the African Revolution,* p. 81.
22. *The Wretched of the Earth,* p. 40.
23. Woddis, p. 82.
24. Arendt, pp. 12, 65, 71. (See under "Related Works.")

25. Arendt, p. 53.
26. *The Wretched of the Earth,* pp. 86, 94.
27. *The Wretched of the Earth,* p. 61.
28. *The Wretched of the Earth,* p. 61.
29. Geismar, p. 144.
30. *The Wretched of the Earth,* p. 96.
31. *The Wretched of the Earth,* p. 94.
32. Gendzier, p. 196.
33. *The Wretched of the Earth,* p. 175.
34. *The Wretched of the Earth,* p. 129.
35. *The Wretched of the Earth,* p. 109.
36. Said, *Culture and Imperialism,* pp. 272, 273. (See under "Related Works.")
37. *The Wretched of the Earth,* p. 152.
38. *The Wretched of the Earth,* p. 175.
39. *The Wretched of the Earth,* pp. 152, 153.
40. *The Wretched of the Earth,* pp. 164, 165.
41. *A Dying Colonialism,* p. 60n.
42. *The Wretched of the Earth,* p. 182.
43. *Toward the African Revolution,* p. 94.
44. *The Wretched of the Earth,* p. 170.
45. *The Wretched of the Earth,* p. 181–82.
46. *The Wretched of the Earth,* p. 189.
47. *The Wretched of the Earth,* p. 99.
48. Samuel P. Huntington, "The Clash of Civilizations," *Foreign Affairs,* 72.3 (1993).
49. Said, *Culture and Imperialism,* pp. 26, 265. (See under "Related Works.")

Bibliography

BOOKS BY FRANTZ FANON

Black Skin, White Masks. New York: Grove Press, 1967.
A Dying Colonialism. New York: Grove Press, 1965.
Toward the African Revolution. New York: Grove Press, 1967.
The Wretched of the Earth. New York: Grove Press, 1963.

BOOKS ON FRANTZ FANON

Bulhan, Hussein Abdilahi. *Frantz Fanon and the Psychology of Oppression.* New York: Plenum Press, 1985.
Caute, David. *Fanon.* London: Fontana/Collins, 1970.
Fontenot, Chester J., Jr. *Frantz Fanon.* Lincoln: University of Nebraska Press, 1979.
Geismar, Peter. *Fanon.* New York: Dial Press, 1971.
Gendzier, Irene. *Frantz Fanon: A Critical Study.* London: Wildwood House, 1973.
Hansen, Emmanuel. *Frantz Fanon: Social and Political Thought.* Columbus: Ohio State University Press, 1977.
Jinadu, L. Adele. *Fanon: In Search of the African Revolution.* London: Kegan Paul International, 1986.
Perinbam, Marie B. *Holy Violence: Frantz Fanon—An Intellectual Biography.* Washington, D.C.: Three Continents Press, 1982.
Woddis, Jack. *New Theories of Revolution: A Commentary on the Thought of Frantz Fanon, Regis Debray and Herbert Marcuse.* New York: International Publishers, 1972.
Zahar, Renate. *Frantz Fanon: Colonialism and Alienation.* New York: Monthly Review Press, 1974.

FILM

The Battle of Algiers. Dir. G. Pontecorvo. Italy, 1966.

ARTICLES AND BOOK CHAPTERS ON FRANTZ FANON

Abrash, Barbara. "Bio-Bibliography: Frantz Fanon." *Africana Library Journal* 2.3 (1971).

Adam, Hussein M. "Fanon as a Democratic Theorist." *African Affairs* 92.4 (1993).

———. "Frantz Fanon: His Understanding." *Black World* 21.2 (1971).

Armah, Ayi Kwei. "Frantz Fanon: The Awakener." *Negro Digest* 18.12 (1969).

Beckett, Paul A. "Fanon and Sub-Saharan Africa." *Africa Today* 19.2 (1972).

Bhabha, Homi. "Remembering Fanon." Foreword to the British edition of *Black Skin, White Masks*. London: Pluto, 1986.

Blackey, Robert. "Fanon and Cabral: A Contrast in Theories of Revolution for Africa." *Journal of Modern African Studies* 12.2 (1974).

Burke, Edmund. "Frantz Fanon's *The Wretched of the Earth*." *Daedalus* 105.1 (1976).

Fontenot, Chester J., Jr. "Fanon and the Devourers." *Journal of Black Studies* 9.1 (1978).

Forsythe, Dennis. "Frantz Fanon: Black Theoretician." *Black Scholar* 1.5 (1970).

———. "Frantz Fanon: The Marx of the Third World." *Phylon* 34.2 (1973).

Foster, Frances. "The Black and White Masks of Frantz Fanon and Ralph Ellison." *Black Academy Review* 1.4 (1970).

Fox-Genovese, Elizabeth, and Eugene Genovese. "Illusion of Liberation: The Psychology of Colonialism and Revolution in the Work of Octave Mannoni and Frantz Fanon." *Rethinking Marxism*. Ed. Stephen Resnick and Richard Wolff. Brooklyn: Autonomedia, 1985.

Garcia Passalacqua, Juan M. "Two Caribbean World Views: Fanon and Naipul." *Wilson Center Working Papers* 124 (1983).

Gibson, Nigel. "Fanon's Humanism and the Second Independence in Africa." *Africa, Human Rights, and the Global System.* Ed. E. McCarthy-Arnolds, D. R. Penna, D. J. Cruz-Sobrepeña. Westport, CT: Greenwood, 1994.

Grohs, G. K. "Frantz Fanon and the African Revolution." *Journal of Modern African Studies* 6.4 (1968).

Hansen, Emmanuel. "Frantz Fanon: A Bibliographical Essay." *Pan-African Journal* 5 (1970).

———. "Frantz Fanon: Portrait of a Revolutionary Intellectual." *Transition* 9.46 (1974).

———. "Freedom and Revolution in the Thought of Frantz Fanon." *Ufahamu* 7.1 (1976).

Helie-Lucas, Marie-Aimée. "Women, Nationalism and Religion in the Algerian National Liberation Struggle." *Opening the Gates.* Ed. Margot Badran and Miriam Cooke. London: Virago, 1990.

Jackson, Henry F. "Political and Social Ideas of Frantz Fanon: Relevance to Black Americans." *Pan-African Journal* 5 (1970).

Jinadu, L. Adele. "Some Aspects of the Political Philosophy of Frantz Fanon." *African Studies Review* 16.3 (1973).

———. "Some Comments on Frantz Fanon and the Historiography of African Politics." *Journal of Developing Areas* 7.2 (1973).

Jones, John Henry. "On the Influence of Fanon," *Freedomways* 8.3 (1968).

Jones, Robert E. "Garbled Voices from Africa: A Critical Study of Pan-African Spokesmen." *Political Communication and Persuasion* 3.1 (1985).

Lacovia, R. M. "Frantz Fanon: Through European Mirrors." *Black Images* 1 (1972).

Martin, Guy. "Fanon's Continuing Relevance: A Comparative Study of the Political Thought of Frantz Fanon and Thomas Sankara." *Journal of Asian and African Affairs* 5.1 (1993).

———. "Fanon's Relevance to African Contemporary Political Thought." *Ufahamu* 4.3 (1974).

Mutiso, G. M. "Fanon, Kathue and the Failure of the African Revolution." *Black World* 20.7 (1971).

Obiechina, Emmanuel. "Frantz Fanon: The Man and His Works." *Ufahamu* 3.2 (1972).

Perinbam, Marie B. "Frantz Fanon and the Revolutionary Peasantry." *Journal of Modern African Studies* 11.3 (1973).

———. "Parrot or Phoenix: Frantz Fanon's View of the West Indian and Algerian Woman." *Journal of Ethnic Studies* 1.2 (1973).

———. "Violence, Morality and History in the Colonial Syndrome: Frantz Fanon's Perspectives." *Journal of Southern African Affairs* 3.1 (1978).

Pittman, John. "Toward the Eradication of Colonialism." *Political Affairs* 47.2 (1968).

Sartre, Jean-Paul. Preface. *The Wretched of the Earth.* By Frantz Fanon. New York: Grove, 1963.

Smith, Robert C. "Frantz Fanon and the Concept of Colonial Violence." *Black World* 22.7 (1973).

Sonnleitner, Michael W. "Of Logic and Liberation: Frantz Fanon on Terrorism." *Journal of Black Studies* 17.3 (1987).

Sutherland, Marcia E. "Individual Differences in Response to the Struggle for the Liberation of People of African Descent." *Journal of Black Studies* 20.1 (1989).

Turner, Lou. "Frantz Fanon: Soweto and Black American Thought." *Notes and Letters* (1978).

———. "The Marxist-Humanist Legacy of Frantz Fanon." *Notes and Letters* 36.10 (1991).

Walters, Ronald. "Essay-Review of Irene Gendzier's *Frantz Fanon: A Critical Study.*" Black World 24.1 (1974).

Welsh-Asante, Kariamu. "Philosophy and Dance in Africa: The Views of Cabral and Fanon." *Journal of Black Studies* 21.2 (1990).

Wright, Frank. "Frantz Fanon: His Work in Historical Perspective." *Black Scholar* 6.9–10 (1975).

Zolberg, Aristide. "The Americanization of Frantz Fanon." *The Public Interest* 9 (1967).

RELATED WORKS

Amin, Samir. *Eurocentrism.* New York: Monthly Review Press, 1989.

Anderson, Benedict. *Imagined Communities: Reflections on the Origin and Spread of Nationalism.* London: Verso, 1983.

Arendt, Hannah. *On Violence.* New York: Harcourt, Brace & World, 1969.

Bennoune, Karima. "Algerian Women Confront Fundamentalism." *Monthly Review* 46.4 (1994).

Bernal, Martin. *The Fabrication of Ancient Greece, 1785–1985.* Vol. 1 of *Black Athena.* New Brunswick, NJ: Rutgers University Press, 1987.

Blaut, J. M. *The Colonizer's Model of the World: Geographical Diffusionism and Eurocentric History.* New York: Guilford Press, 1993.

Césaire, Aimé. *Discourse on Colonialism.* New York: Monthly Review Press, 1972.

Freire, Paulo. *Pedagogy of the Oppressed.* New York: Herder and Herder, 1971.

Ghalem, Ali. *A Wife for My Son.* Chicago: Banner Press, 1984.

Hall, Stuart. "Negotiating Caribbean Identities." *New Left Review* 209 (1995).

Hobsbawm, Eric, and Terence Ranger, eds. *The Invention of Tradition.* Cambridge: Cambridge University Press, 1983.

James, C. L. R. *C. L. R. James and Revolutionary Marxism: Selected Writings.* Ed. Scott McLemee and Paul LeBlanc. Atlantic Highlands, NJ: Humanities Press, 1994.

Kiernan, Victor G. *The Lords of Human Kind.* Boston: Little, Brown, 1969.

———. *Marxism and Imperialism.* New York: St. Martin's Press, 1975.

Lewis, Gordon K. *Slavery, Imperialism and Freedom.* New York: Monthly Review Press, 1978.

McClintock, Anne. "No Longer in a Future Heaven." *Transition* 51 (1993).

Memmi, Albert. *The Colonizer and the Colonized.* Boston: Beacon Press, 1967.

———. *Dominated Man.* Boston: Beacon Press, 1968.

Ngugi wa Thiong'o. *Decolonizing the Mind.* London: James Currey, 1986.

Raskin, Jonah. *The Mythology of Imperialism.* New York: Random House, 1971.

Said, Edward W. *Culture and Imperialism.* New York: Vintage Books, 1994.

————. *Orientalism.* New York: Vintage Books, 1979.

Sorel, Georges. *Reflections on Violence.* New York: Collier Books, 1961.

Tlemçani, Rachid. *State and Revolution in Algeria.* Boulder, CO: Westview, 1992.

Tlemçani, Rachid, and William W. Hansen. "Development and the State in Post-Colonial Algeria." *Journal of Asian and African Studies* 24.1–2 (1989).

West, Cornel. *The Ethical Dimensions of Marxist Thought.* New York: Monthly Review Press, 1991.

————. *Keeping Faith.* New York: Routledge, 1993.

————. *Race Matters.* New York: Vintage, 1993.

About the Author of
This Guide

William Hansen is a Scholar-in-Residence at Trinity College, Hartford. He was educated at the University of Maryland, the University of London, and Boston University. He has written on the subjects of Leninism, socialism, development theory, and Africa. In 1993, he published an essay with Brigitte Schulz entitled "Colonial Capitalism and Socialism: The Radical Theory of Frantz Fanon," and his *Frantz Fanon: An Introduction* was published in Germany by Decaton Verlag in 1996. He is currently working on an extensive analytical interpretation of Fanon's political thought.

Ordering Information

Grove/Atlantic, Inc. (Grove Press and Atlantic Monthly Press) titles are available from Grove/Atlantic, Inc.'s distributor, Publishers Group West.

For customer service inquiries or to place an order, open an account, or obtain information on terms and conditions, please call our toll-free number, (800) 788-3123, between 9:00 A.M. and 5:30 P.M. PST, Monday through Friday. You may fax orders to us during all hours: (510) 658-1834.

Mail Orders Should Be Sent to:

Grove/Atlantic, Inc.
c/o Publishers Group West
ATTN: Order Department
P.O. Box 8843
Emeryville, CA 94662

Please Ensure that the Following Information Is Included On All Mail Orders:

1) Ship-to and bill-to addresses
2) Account number
3) Telephone and fax numbers
4) Purchase order or reference number
5) Special shipping instructions (if any)
6) Back order preferences (if any)
7) Quantity and titles of each item ordered

All orders are F.O.B. Hayward, CA.

To open an account with Publishers Group West, please submit a completed and signed credit application, including a copy of your state resale or tax exempt certificate.

Academic Examination and Desk Copies

Paperback examination and desk copies are available to professors and teachers considering a title for course adoption. All requests must be submitted in writing on university letterhead or the appropriate AAP form. All requests must include the course's title, beginning date, approximate enrollment size, as well as the name of the college store that will be placing the order. To help defray shipping and handling charges, $4.00 for the first book and 75¢ for each additional book ordered must accompany your request.

Please send your request to:

Grove/Atlantic, Inc.
c/o Publishers Group West
ATTN: Academic Sales Department
P.O. Box 8843
Emeryville, CA 94662

Hardcover editions are not available gratis for examination and desk-copy review.

Note to Individuals

If you are unable to obtain a Grove Press or Atlantic Monthly Press book through your customary source (and most booksellers will special-order a title they do not have in stock), you may order directly from the publisher by calling our toll-free number, (800) 788-3123, and using American Express, MasterCard, or Visa or by mailing your order directly to Publishers Group West, P.O. Box 8843, Emeryville, CA 94662; please enclose $4.00 for the first book and 75¢ for each additional book ordered for shipping and handling. Please also include the applicable state and city sales tax if you live in California or New York.

Pricing Information

Prices listed are always the suggested cover price. All resellers are free to charge any price they choose for books. All prices, publication dates, and specifications are subject to change.